A Wartime
In Hudder

A Wartime Boyhood In Huddersfield

By Russell Jones

Edited by
Georgina Hutchison

Cover Design by
Tracey Barker

First published 2021

Early Days In Birchencliffe

I was born on 13th January 1932 and spent my babyhood at Longwood. When I was still very young, my mother and father moved to Birchencliffe, a village on the outskirts of Huddersfield, built on a rocky outcropping. One of my main memories of the place is near Halifax Road, where about twenty steep steps led up to what was locally known as the cliff, and from a six-foot viewing space guarded by iron rails, one could stand and look out over passing traffic – what little there was in my early days.

I can envisage the lane leading to where I lived; to the left are cottages, and to the right a small stony yard with more cottages around it. Walking on, we come to Briar Fold. The first house to the left, facing onto the lane, was number 26. The next, facing onto the fold, was our house – number 24. The Harrisons, including my friend Arthur, lived at number 22 and below them was a pile of stone, the remains of a house. A lane led to Birchencliffe Hill Road, and there you would find number 18 where the Hinchcliffes lived, including twins Paul and Pauline. Arthur's Uncle Willie lived at 16. At the end of the fold, an opening led back out onto Briar Lane (numbers 48, 46, 44 and 42 were here) and then there was a ginnel leading to the back lane.

Illustration 1: Our first house at Longwood: From left, my sister Audrey held by my mum Edna Jones; me held by my Auntie Gwendoline Mary Roebuck (neé Lewis, wife of Harold);my Uncle Harold Roebuck. In the doorway, you can just make out a figure – most likely my dad, Robert Jones.

The father of the Hinchcliffe twins, Harry, worked with my dad in the clay quarry situated in the field adjacent to Briar Lane – a site which is now home to a large garden centre. Harry was the shot firer in the quarry and my dad dug the clay and loaded it onto small trucks via a double rail, sending it down to the brick yard. The rail ran through a tunnel under Birchencliffe Hill Road, just above Ben Machini's ice cream factory and just opposite Barker's farm. My dad, Robert Edward Jones, also helped to make the bricks. I well remember him coming home all covered in dried clay after work.

What a contrast to my best clothes on a Sunday, when I went off to the Wesleyan Chapel in Lindley, my attendance book all neatly stamped with stars! I was told a prize could be mine with regular attendance. During the week I attended Holly Bank Road School – I remember the road, all grey cobbles with two sets of tram lines, and I also remember my teacher, Miss Butterfield.

Arthur Harrison, my friend and neighbour, was in a higher class than me. One day we were walking home from school throwing stones and Arthur broke a house window. I said it was him, and he said it was me. When I got home, I was in disgrace – and the window had to be paid for! At the end of the fold onto Briar Lane, which was very stony, stood a gas lamp post which was lit by a lamp-lighter. It was good for climbing up to get into the quarry field where we were not supposed to go. Walking up the lane to the top right, Arthur and I would pass the back of A.G. Boyes garage where there were old tyres and engines. The garage were agents for Standard and Triumph motors,

Illustration 2: A view of Prince Royd at Birchencliffe

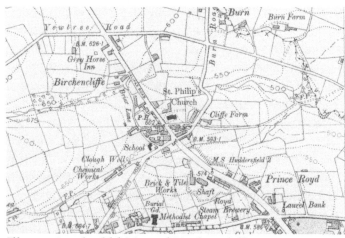

Illustration 3: Old Map of Birchencliffe

and in later years they moved to the top of the (then new) ring road in Huddersfield. Further on, we'd come to the entrance to the cricket club on our left – the pitch was good for digging hairy nuts.

Down the lane was a place we knew as the Dodge – a wide stream with bushes lining both banks, then walls at either side and big trees overhanging the stream. It was the perfect place for adventure and for getting wet shoes.

We had to keep a sharp eye out for older boys who also used to go into the woods where we climbed trees – it was keep away from them or get a thumping. There was one tree down by the river bank where we would tie a rope to the thickest branch and make a swing that would go out over the river – the further, the better, taking turns to see who could swing the furthest. Another game we had was to put your foot on a log, not moving it at all, and see who could throw a knife nearest to it. This game was banned after the knife went into Willie's foot. He finished up with cat gut stitches. We used to wear old knives down on a stone to balance them; we used anything – old carving knives, bread knives, scraps of metal. Grimescar woods was a favourite playground, fishing for sticklebacks in the stream, always on the lookout for German agents. And on summer days, with two slices of bread and sugar, and a bottle of water, I could stay in Greenhead park nearly all day.

I remember sunny days, walking with my mam, my dad and and my sister down Burn Road. My dad was a tall man with boots and dark trousers, a white, collarless shirt and his flat cap pulled down over his right ear. He would hoist us all over the farm gate and we'd go down the path to the part of Barker's Fields known locally as the Cat Grave or the Cat – the stream which runs down through Birkby and on to the River Colne (the Dodge was further up this same stream). Off came our shoes and socks so we could dam the stream, then we fished for sticklebacks by hand, and sailed boats made of sticks and leaves. We had to avoid cow clap though, which was in abundance. On being a good lad, I might get a lolly from Frank Howe's shop which stood on the corner of Birchencliffe Hill, fronting onto Halifax Road.

My dad once took me to the cinematograph in the church hall in Lindley. It was one penny for me to get in, and magic to see my dad's favourite funny man, Buster Keaton. Then there were Ben Turpin, Harold Lloyd, Charlie Chaplin – all the stars of silent film.

In my school days, I passed regularly up the hill to Lindley, with an old blacksmith shop on the left and a bicycle shop on the right (which was still there fifty years later). On the corner of Holly Bank Road was a sweet shop and I always had a look in the window, even if I had no money. There were all kinds of boiled sweets and toffees in jars, and a big red tin with a lion on it that contained hundreds and thousands – a ha'p'orth got us half a bag full.

After school, we'd go on to the rec. At the top were a set of three individual swings, a see-saw, a roundabout, and – my favourite – the big swing, an item long gone from children's playgrounds. It seated six, or eight at a squeeze, with a big boy stood at each end doing the work of pulling the big swing up as high as it would go. I thought to myself, one day I'll stand and work the swing. I was always late home.

Illustration 4: Clockwise from far left: Evan Evans (my step-grandad), Robert (Bob) Jones (my dad), Edna Roebuck (my mum), Cyril Saxley (best man), Alfred Roebuck (my Granddad), Lillian Roebuck (my aunty, bridesmaid) and Evelyn (bridesmaid). This was taken in 1928, when my parents got married.

It may have been around this time that my mother (Edna's) illness came to my notice. Of course, I did not know what it was, but I saw the small set of brass scales being taken out of a box and small portions of food being weighed in the mornings; a test-tube with a wire handle being warmed on the gas ring and my mother injecting her thigh with a needle. Type 1 Diabetes, I later learned.

Yet, as a young boy, I was still busy having fun. I remember waiting for Sammy to come – the clip-clop on the road and then the clatter over stones in Briar Lane then the pony would appear pulling Ben Machini's ice cream float. It was a two-wheeled cart of red, gold and blue with a canopy with a fancy golden point on top. Sat beside the ice-wrapped drum of ice-cream was Sammy with his fair hair and smiling face. He sold the best ice cream cornets and sandwiches ever produced and I always thought he would have looked good in a naval uniform. I wondered, back then, where he came from and where he went.

Illustration 5: Ben Machini's Ice Cream Carts

I really looked forward to Sundays after school, and if we were going out, I left my best clothes on. If it was rainy, we'd take a tram ride to town and then another to Longwood. If we had no tram money, we walked to Grandma Roebuck's (my mother's mother) - it was up the hill to Lindley, up Cowcraiks Road (always full of cow pats from farmers driving herds of cows down the road), then about a mile to Salendine Nook over three stiles across fields. This brought us on to Longwood Edge which overlooked Milnsbridge, and the whole of Golcar, with Scapegoat Hill above and beyond in the distance. We would turn left down a stony road for about three hundred yards, then take a right turn down a very stony wide road with high rocks to the right and a sheer drop of twenty feet on the left (with more rocks at the bottom).

Illustration 6: View from Longwood Edge

As the ground levelled out, some steep stone steps through a gap between houses took us onto High Street, and here lived my Grandma, at number 2. She had a block of two toilets across the yard, with a low wall to the right. A steep, stony lane alongside it was flanked by big trees and a high wall. Beyond the high wall was my Granddad's allotment and his hen run.

The door to the hen run was halfway down the lane – it was a big black one with a sneck lock on it. The bottom of the lane led onto the cobbled road to Paddock and Huddersfield. My Grandma's house (which would, these days, be called a cottage) had two or maybe three bedrooms, one living room, and a cellar at the back with a great stone slab on top of two stone wall supports. In the corner of the room was a stone sink with one brass cold tap, and in the middle of the room was a big, scrubbed white table with four or five chairs – a rocking chair was my favourite. My Granddad would be across the yard looking across Golcar with an old pair of opera glasses. My Grandma would be making the dinner.

My Auntie Lillian would be out walking. My uncles, Harold and Walter, would both be in bed. Harold would be first up, to send me down to the little shop in Dods Lea with money for five woodbines and a lolly. The shop, which was back down the big steps, opened for an hour on Sundays. I remember also walking with my dad, Granddad and two uncles on High Street, through small hen runs in the front of the cottages, through a passage to the Dusty Miller public house. The men went in, but I had to sit outside with a lemonade. Looking into the pub, I could see brass rails round the bar and spittoons and sawdust on the floor.

To one side was a black leaded fireplace and barrels were lined behind the bar.

Illustration 7: Alfred and Jane Roebuck, my Grandma and Granddad

After the drink I would run back to Grandma's, the men would arrive back and Grandma Roebuck would bang a big spoon on a plate or tin and shout, 'dinner's ready, Yorkshires are out.' Then we all sat down to the big scrubbed white table for dinner with vegetables out of the big garden down the lane.

Sometimes I would go with Granddad up the steep lane at the back of the house and on up Longwood Edge. I had a shovel and a bucket to collect horse manure – there were always lots of riders and horses and carts up there. My Granddad had to carry the bucket when it was full. On summer days, we'd walk on Snow Lea, past the Church and its yard where my Uncle Harold now lies, on past the big house and the cottages through the fields – and then back to no.2 High Street for tea. It's funny, but I can never remember what we had for tea except for tomatoes and lettuce. After tea the table was cleared, a tasselled table cloth was put on and out came a pack of cards. While cards were played I was given a book, and sometimes the rocking chair. The book was Grimms Fairy Tales, in every other page a pressed flower – ferns, leaves, grasses – which I had to carefully remove and place back when the page was read. My favourite stories were The Valiant Little Tailor and Rumpelstiltskin. The talk at the table was of people and places and work and, later, the forthcoming war. When it was dark we all went home by tram down to town, followed by another tram to Birchencliffe.

One special day my dad came home in a 1936 Ford 8. The registration number was AUA 835. I think this happened when he changed jobs, now working for Sharrats Brick Works. He said we could all sit in the

12

Illustration 8: Sharrats Brick Works

Illustration 9: Sharrats Brick Works

car but that we had not to stand on the leather seats. I think, in retrospect, the car belonged to his manager. My dad had his driving licence from being 18, and later had a motorbike and sidecar.

Sharrats Brick Works was situated on the Halifax Road to Elland (called the Ainleys). At the bottom of the hill, just past the pub on the right and through a passage, lived my Grandma and Granddad Evans. Next door lived my dad's sister, my Aunty Marie. In Elland, my dad was known as Bob Evans (rather than Bob Jones) on account of his step-father, Evan Evans's, surname.

Just opposite the pub stood Elland forge. It was a big one with maybe three or four farriers and two furnaces going. I liked to walk up there and watch. There were always horses in, being shod, sparks flying all over the place and iron being hammered on the anvil. I always thought it would be good if I could be a blacksmith.

I remember Grandma Evans's house – a black leaded fireplace, bright blazing fire and Granddad sat cleaning his boots. For tea we had bacon and tomatoes. But I did not like going to school in Elland (as I sometimes had to). Prayers before classes? Some wonder I did not learn much!

I used to go next door to Aunty Marie's. Uncle Bert came home during work-time, just for a pot of tea, and had to stand in the doorway or sit on newspaper on a buffet. Uncle Bert (Herbert) was a chimney sweep – I can see him now, a small, thin man in a flat cap, smiling face, as black as a crow. At least he left his brushes and canes outside on the step! After his drink, off he went to clean more chimneys – sweeps were always in demand as every house had a coal fire. I still hear the coal man, driving his wagon slowly down the road shouting 'Coal!' at the top of his voice – 'Three bags, Missus,' and crash, down would go the hundred weight bags on top of the coal hole down the passage, and then a clatter as the coal thundered into the cellar.

Grandma Evans talked in a heavy Scouse accent, so later I could recognize a Liverpool accent. She used to keep her money in her stocking top. Sending me for shopping, she would lift her skirt and take a small purse out of her stocking top and tell me I could also have a pennyworth of sweets or a lolly, or give me money for the pictures.

The Palladium was the picture house – known locally as Town Hall. I had to go with Aunty Marie. I saw Snow White there, and Hellza Poppin and comedy films of the day. My introduction to the silver screen was a real treat for me.

Illustration 10: Elland, a view of Huddersfield Road

My Granddad Evans would sometimes take me to his work – he was a night-watchman in a mill so I presume he was past retirement age. The mill was across the road and up a street, and he had his own little corner with one electric light and an easy chair. He would sit with his pipe, papers and books all night long, his time broken only by checking on doors and machinery at hourly intervals. When I got out of bed next morning, he would be sat in front of the blazing fire polishing brass or his boots, the fireplace itself freshly black-leaded and gleaming.

Illustration 11: Elland, a view opposite Grandma Evans's house on the Huddersfield/Halifax Road.

My Time At Thistle Street

In 1939 my family moved from Birchencliffe to no.2. Thistle Street, off Leeds Road in Huddersfield. It was a grey cobbled road with three gas lamps tended by a lamp lighter who came round at dawn and dusk and also cleaned the reflectors. But at the outbreak of war, the lamp lighter became redundant as no light was to be shown at all. At the top of the road on the left hand corner was a public house – The Spinners – and at the bottom of the road on the left hand corner was another – The Weavers. Turning left off Thistle Street itself, there was a row of council houses set in a crescent, then three more which are still there today.

The bottom of Thistle Street brought you to St Andrews Road, and turning right, you'd pass the bottom of Glendennings Mill, with Blamires Mill to the left and the town rubbish dump on the right. There was also what we called the Destructors, a big building with a giant pit incinerator which was kept burning night and day, only stopping to renew the kiln bricks. Gasworks street, where the town's gas was made, was a turning off to the right. Going further on brought you to Turnbridge, and row after row of terrace houses, the streets all named after flowers.

If you turned left off Thistle Street onto St Andrews Road, there was Town Avenue which led to

Illustration 12: Aerial View of Thistle Street, the sunlit road in the left-hand corner of the picture. The Spinners Arms pub is visible at bottom left. The Jones home was on the right-hand side of Thistle Street.

Illustration 13: The Spinners Arms

Illustration 14: The Weavers public house

Illustration 15: Aerial View of area around Thistle Street – St Andrews Road runs from bottom middle to top right corner. Thistle Street is visible as a left-hand turn off St Andrews Road. The curving road running across the top of the picture is Leeds Road.

Huddersfield Town Football Ground, which had allotments next to it. Then there was a football field with a high railway sleeper fence, but this was short-lived as it became a coal yard in 1940. I remember a high-fenced lane, the River Colne down on the right, and the back gardens of houses leading towards Bradley Mills.

At the top of Thistle Street was Leeds Road, and across it was Hillhouse Lane leading to Great Northern Street, and the railway and tram/bus sheds. Also on the other side of Leeds Road was Beaumont Street, and my school, and the Monday Market. All this area that I have described was my playground in the war and post-war years.

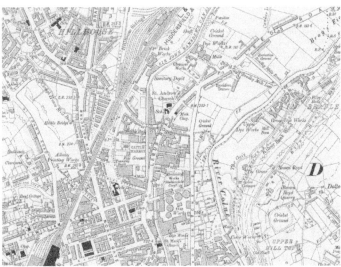

Illustration 16: Map of Leeds Road area of central Huddersfield. Thistle Street is in the centre of this image

When I started junior school my mam took me for the first day, then I walked up on my own. I would not walk with my sisters. I remember going out of the house to play and being stopped by a boy about my size and age with a shock of ginger hair. He asked me if I had any brothers or sisters, and if I knew the name of those hills over there. He was Colin Ackroyd though I called him Acky and he called me Russ or Rusty.

We became good friends and school mates. Wagons would come and tip great heaps of coal outside the mill gates which had to be wheeled in to feed the furnace for the mill machines. It was good fun to run up and down these till we were chased off by the men who had to shovel it up. When we got our gas masks, we had to practice putting them on at home and at school. If you blow hard when you have one on, you make farting noises out of the rubber around your face, which made everybody laugh. We also got given round, white badges which smelled funny, but which glowed in the dark. We were told to eat plenty of carrots to see in the blackout.

Black sticky tape was bought to stick on the window panes to stop flying splinters, and it was down to us lads to collect as much scrap metal as we could find. We went knocking on doors for old pans, rusty buckets and lumps of metal, and piled it all up in the street for the wagon that came.

Nothing could be wasted. Swill bins were bought and any mouldy or uneaten food had to be sent for animal food. All the metal railings were cut down and even unwanted dogs had to go, except for working dogs and Alsations needed for war work. Among all the people I knew, I only knew one dog and it belonged to Acky's dad. It was a terrier – a very obedient dog who would walk at his heel as he went up the street holding the small of his back. Acky's dad had been in the 1914 war and finished with shell shrapnel near his back bone. It eased his pain to hold his back when walking.

Ration books were issued, which did not mean much to me – except for sweets. We called them spice, but they vanished from the shops, leaving cough sweets, some mints and fiery little black imps. Home guards were formed and air raid wardens came into being; fire buckets and stirrup pumps were issued; sand bags, heavy curtains and black blinds were bought. Anderson shelters were given to people with gardens and we all helped dig holes at least six feet deep. Best of all, in our back yard we had a brick shelter with a concrete roof, perfect for a gang hut. There was one in the crescent round the corner too.

We got to know the outline and shape of German bombers and fighters – Hienkels, Dorniers, Messerschmidts, Stukas; in fact, every plane the Gerrys made. We made bows, and arrows with nails tied on, catapults, sling shots, kitchen knives – anything to fight with – and vowed to fight. There was Keith (Fish), Tom, Acky, Ken, Brod, Pete and George. We used to play with Tommy Ryan, but he said we had to pinch something out of Woolworths to be in his gang. My mam said I had not to play with him as his family did not work. He used to go out with Jack Gash, a thief who finally got the birch when he was 18.

Everyone walked to school, up St Andrews Road.

On cold days we warmed our backs on the furnace steel doors, then it was up Gasworks Street and on to school. I never had an overcoat, just a jacket and cap, and when it was raining my mam would stand at the door and shout 'walk under t' wall lad'. It worked if you walked close to a lee wall. We had jam bread, or bread and sugar with tea for breakfast, and sugar in paper with a piece of rhubarb for school. Sometimes it might be cocoa and sugar, or a carrot.

Illustration 17: A view from Gasworks Street

Up Hillhouse Lane, over the canal bridge, we would look for barges drawn by horses. They plied none-stop, since there was no petrol for wagons, and were mostly piled with coal. On up through the yard to Great Northern Street (later the scene for murder by the Yorkshire Ripper), we'd pass the slaughter house, the cattle market, the bus sheds, the market place, and granite-cobbled Beaumont Street with its railway lines up the middle. The Beaumont Street flyer, a humpy saddle-back steam engine, used to ply twice a day, moving coal from the railway sidings at the top to the gasworks at the bottom – maybe four or six trucks full - then back again in the afternoon with the empties. It would be accompanied by two men with red and green flags. When we were out of school, we'd hitch a lift on the buffers and the men would shout 'You're going to kill yourselves!' and chase us off. I once put a halfpenny on the line. I kept that flattened coin for years.

Illustration 18: The Beaumont Street Flyer

Along Beaumont Street there was a shoddy mill that took up all the left-hand side. Outside on the causeway there were always great big bales of shoddy waiting to be taken in. The bales were just an 8 foot square bag of sacking secured on two sides by wooden skewers.

Illustration 19: The Railway Sidings

Illustration 20: Another view of the Beaumont Street Flyer

We all used to dash out of school, straight over the wall, down the street and pile onto the bales until the mill workers could chase us off. Sometimes, we stole the skewers.

Then down the steps to the canal bank, we would throw stones in the cut. Just over the bridge on the left, there was a wholesale meat shop where you could see lines of sides of beef waiting to be collected. One day a van had gone through the wall into the canal. They brought a big crane to lift it out, but a chain broke and it crashed back in. It cost me fifty lines as I was late for school after watching.

Every day was an adventure. I went to school with my jacket pockets stuffed with all sorts – string, rubber bands, shrapnel, bullet shells, spent automatic bullets, cigarette packets... When the Americans came, all these fancy packets were coming – Camels and other brands. The exchange rate for them in school was high. Anything was up for barter or currency, even nails, because during the war everything was in short supply. Pre-war comics were the best barter – 1932 to 1938, at least ten pages in those – but the very best was pieces of perspex from a Spitfire or pieces from German planes that had been shot down. These would be brought back by friends and relatives in the forces who were home on leave. The war touched us, even at home. I regularly saw school mates called out and given a message – relative killed in action – and then they went home crying. We saw lots of drawn curtains in those days, giving that same message.

We got hold of Sten gun bullets by stealth. There was a firing range across the canal from Canker Lane. It was used by both the army and home guard, and was surrounded with barbed wire and signs with skull and crossbones saying 'W.D. Keep Out.' The best time to get in was just before dusk. Me and Stringer ran down Diamond Street past the old brick kilns, over the steaming ashes dump and across two fields, carrying a piece of plank to throw over the wire. It was a dodgy job to balance and walk over the wire, but then it was down to the butts – a big bank of sand and earth which held the targets – to dig out the bullets by hand. Then we were over the other side, up a big steel gate, across the cut and home through Canker Lane. By this time it would be dark. It wasn't too bad if it was a clear night, but otherwise, with not one single light on, it was pitch black – unless there was moonlight, and we liked this even less! We called it a bomber's moon, and they'd come at about two in the morning. We liked the cloud and mist – it was harder for the navigators and those aiming the bombs.

Everybody wanted a commando knife. I got one, a big one, but the handle had come off. I don't know what I gave for it, but somebody had brought it back and I thought I'm having this! I tried to make a handle but it wasn't very good.

Monday was a good day, even at school. The Monday market was on the lump next to the school. The town bus depot opposite was always busy, and added to that was the cattle market to the left on the same day. The slaughter house was next to it, and as the farmers drove the beasts from the rail yards in town, the cows and bulls would smell the blood and set off mooing and howling. Added to the noise of all the stall holders shouting their wares, it was a sound I've never forgotten. We could hear the auctioneers

Illustration 21: The Monday Market

Illustration 22: Another view of the Monday Market

shouting the price of the cattle.

At dinnertime, I always wanted a fork with a crown on it, and you had to be in the front ten to get the brown sauce or there was none left. A typical dinner was mashed turnip, corned beef, and cabbage, then sponge and a thin custard. I did not like ground rice, but we were told to eat all our food as some of our soldiers were going hungry.

One day, word came that a bull was loose on the road. Acky, Stringer and me dashed out over the school wall and on to Great Northern Street. Men with ropes, nets and a shot gun had got the bull up against a wall in Hillhouse Lane. There was great excitement, but we were told to bugger off out of the way. Before they could get a rope on it, the bull charged back on the road, cheered on by us. Once again it was cornered, in a lane at the side of a wood yard. Our offers of help were declined in no uncertain terms. The bull got a rope put through its nose ring and was tied to a wagon to be dragged to the cattle market. And I was nearly late back at school again.

We had a bank book and every week on a certain day you took twopence or threepence or sometimes just a penny, and had it put in your bank book. We came in one day and we were all queueing up to put our money in and word came round – Tindall's in, he's got a pound! And everyone wanted to look at this pound note. We'd never seen one and everyone went to see it. Teacher had to shout orders at us, there was pandemonium over it.

Our favourite place for dinnertime break was to walk up to Northgate near the Majestic cinema and watch the coopers at work making barrels for wine, ale, whiskey and all sorts of fluids. I remember the workmen in their leather aprons, trimming the staves, putting the steel hoops on by hammer, dropping a fire in the bottom, making the barrel watertight. One day we saw a cooper who must have finished his apprenticeship being hoisted up by all the other men. They dropped him in the barrel then poured all sorts on him – oil, tar, saw dust. The man got out filthy but laughing. It was all part of learning the trade.

Illustration 23: The Majestic cinema

On winter nights I would read comic papers – Dandy, and Beano – and Film Fun, portraying stars of the cinema like Laurel and Hardy. Later on, I read papers for older boys – Hotspur, Rogan flying his Spitfire and shooting up the Germans, The Wizard (starring the hero Wilson). The first book I read was Just William, out of the library, followed by all the series. Then I read Robert Louis Stevenson's Treasure Island.

Illustration 24: Beaumont Street School

Having read my weekly copy of the Beano, I would dash across Thistle Street to a friend's house to swap comics. This halted a bit when we got a radio. Up to this point, all I had was a 'cat's whisker' or crystal set to pick up radio waves, and all I could get was Germany Calling, and Lord Haw Haw, the propaganda voice. But on the radio there was home service for the home front forces, and overseas music. They used to blast it through loud speakers in the factories and the girls doing war work, making guns, tanks, planes and ammunition, all used to sing along to the popular songs of the day – Don't Sit Under The Apple Tree, Run Rabbit Run...

But my favourite was Music Hall – Arthur Askey, George Formby. Max Miller, Gert and Daisy (real names Elsie and Doris Waters), Norman Evans,

ITMA, Tommy Handley, Frank Randle, Nat Jackley, Leslie Hutchison, Paul Robson, Cavan O'Connor, Peter Cavanagh, Three Monarchs, Vera Lynn, Ann Shelton, Gracie Fields, Tessie O'Shea, Albert Whelan, Sandy Powell, Ali Bongo, the Northern Dance Orchestra, Squadronairs, Billy Cotton, Victor Sylvester, Major Glen Miller's army air force band, the Philharmonic Orchestra, Gilbert and Sullivan, and all the big-band records from America – Benny Goodman, Duke Ellington, Louie Armstrong, Spike Jones and his city slickers...

On Saturdays I was sent to the Co-op for rations, along with a list and the ration books (sometimes five of them). Of course, there was always a queue, especially at the butchers, and sometimes men would jump in front of me and I would shout murder, and the butcher would come out and make the queue jumpers go to the back. Because meat was in short supply, last in line got sausages, corned beef and bones, all of which I liked. My mam would boil the bones with onion, carrot and turnip. It made a good stew with some corned beef. But my favourite on Saturdays was pork pies and mash. I would be up early and join the queue at Hallas's butchers on Northgate for four four-penny pies and one six-penny pie.

In the afternoon, if I had some money, I'd go with the boys up to the Regent picture house. It was threepence, or best seats for fourpence, and was great fun, packed with just kids, and with pea shooters, elastic bands and pellets the order of the day.

They showed serial films, and just when they got to the most exciting part – Flash Gordon being shot by ray gun, or the Durango kid hanging off a cliff top – it

Illustration 25: A contemporary shop front, this one was on Bradford Road.

was cut and the words 'See in this theatre next week' came up. The next week of course, the shot missed, or Durango was thrown a rope, but you still had to be there.

I would also go with my school mates from Brackenhall to the Rialto in Sheepridge. The same stars were on there, plus cartoons, and all the cowboys – Gene Autry, hoppalong Cassidy, the Cisco Kid, Roy Rogers with his famous white horse Trigger. Everyone remembers Trigger (his statue still stands in Hollywood) but few remember the dog's name – Bullet. I enjoyed Zorro as well.

To get money for the pictures I would knock on doors to run errands – take bottles back, chop wood, scrub steps – anything for a tanner for the flicks. I have no complaints about my life, or the poverty of those times, but I have had to work hard for every penny I have got, and many don't appreciate what that is like. I remember my dad parking the Flying Standard Nine at the front of the house in Thistle Street, and all the lads came to look at it – we even got to sit in it. It made me so proud of my dad. Around 2001, I met two women who I knew as girls when they lived in my street. I said hello, and one said 'Oh, it's Russell Jones.' We got talking and one of them said to me, 'You were a mucky, scruffy lot.' I said, 'Maybe, but we were the only house in the whole street to have a car and you were a stuck-up b****.' And I walked on. We went to Bridlington in that car, I remember, camping with a bell tent.

Some dinnertimes a few of us would go up town to the Wholesale market to see what we could scrounge out of the empty boxes, like discarded, part-rotten fruit. My most valuable possession was my pen-knife and with it I could easily cut out the bad. I'd find apples, oranges, pears, carrots, turnip, even potatoes, but while we were up town, we had to keep our eyes peeled for red caps (from another school) or a fight would ensue. Black eyes, fat lips and torn clothes would get us into trouble both at home and at school, since torn clothes could not easily be replaced. As well as finding discarded fruit, we used to take all the boxes that it came in - we'd whip them straight out of the big market doors and pile them outside the school wall so we could use them as firewood.

Shortages meant holes in shoes or pumps were a regular thing, and my dad showed me how to cobble my shoes. Using four or five nails, you'd nail a piece of leather slightly larger than the sole to a cast iron last. Then the leather was cut to the size of the sole and attached with nails all round the edge. A rasp was used to file the edges smooth, segs were put on the toes and heels, and blacking was put round the edge of the new sole. The leather in wartime was inferior and soon wore away, and you had to make sure there were no nails stuck up inside the shoe.

You could get clogs easier, though. I wore them for school, and they were good for your feet. They had thick wooden soles and iron bands – like a horseshoe on the bottom. You could make sparks with them by kicking against the floor. But the clogs collected snow – it stuck to the bottoms making them like platforms!

I went to a friends house once and his mother looked at me in my pumps, with my sole flapping off, and she brought me in. She said 'try these on' and gave me a pair of leather shoes. All leather, and they fit me! I said 'these are lovely'. She said, 'you can have them.' They were like brand new, all polished up. I thought, oh crikey, I daren't go out in these, they're Sunday shoes, but she insisted, 'you wear them, throw those other things away.'

Everything was needed, and not a thing was wasted in those days. A good sideline for me was pulling rusty nails out of old wood and hammering them straight for sale or swap, and putting segs onto leather-soled shoes to stop them wearing out, or putting irons onto clogs. In 1941, it felt like all I was doing was collecting metal from all over, pulling nails out of wood, as metal was needed for the war effort. They brought a real Hurricane into St George's Square as an attraction to get donations in. Another time they brought a sea mine, with a slot in the top for people to put money in.

I remember during the war years there was hardly

any traffic, because there was no petrol except for commercial and people on war work (and, of course, the top people with loads of cash). If you got caught using red petrol (commercial fuel) you could be fined heavily, or jailed, as it was badly needed at the front. I remember hearing the banging noise from Moorhouse Boilers, but we never knew what they were making there. We knew that 'Careless talk costs lives' and so no one talked about war work.

My dad was a gambler and when he had money he was always studying form. He would write out his bets and wait for me coming in, then he'd give me the money wrapped in the bet paper. He'd tell me to call at certain houses to see if they had any bets to go to the bookie as I would get a good tip if we had winners. The bets were usually threepence, sixpence or a shilling. I would run (I never walked) up Leeds Road just past Fitzwilliam Street, past the pub, three shops, a barbers, Dransfield's paper shop (where I later got a job as a paper boy), until I got to the cobbler's shop.

I never knew his name – he was just the cobbler or the bookie. The shop was something else – it looked like it had not been cleaned up for years. Leather pairings were ankle-deep on the floor, and there were dozens of iron lasts, tools, blacking, browning and sheets of leather. There were belt-driven tools worked off a shaft powered by an old electric motor, and the place was littered with boots, shoes and clogs of every size. The bookie sat on a stool knocking nails into a sole with a rasp. He took the bets, looked at the names on the slips, stuck them on a stand nail and said 'Ok lad, if there is anything to come back, come to the house'. At that time, this was illegal, but the police turned a blind eye as they also used runners to place bets.

After the races had been run, if there were smiles all round, someone would come and fetch me – 'Russell, your dad wants you.' I knew it was to get the winnings. Then it was up to the bookie's house – up on Northumberland Street, through a passage round the back. I'd get called into a room where the bookie sat at a table with his ledgers, the winning bets all wrapped up. I would have to check my dad's, as he had his money reckoned up to the penny.

My dad was very good following the form of horses. He used to tell me that as a boy, he would sneak into Aintree to watch the races and see the punters and the touts. During summer, he said, he would go swimming in the Manchester-Liverpool ship canal

At the first snow of winter, the sledges were brought out. I had to make my own. It was not very good as it had solid wooden runners and, even after polishing and waxing, it wasn't very fast – even down what we called the death track on Kilner Bank, where there weren't even trees to stop you. Stockings were the order of the day – we'd cut off the bottoms and pull them up the leg to cover the gap between socks and short trousers. We didn't have long trousers until the age of fourteen. We wore socks on our hands to keep them warm. If we were at school when the snow started, we would watch and hope it came thick and fast. When the bell went, we were out like bullets over the school wall, home for tea as fast as possible, and then out again, followed by shouts of 'Be in for nine o'clock!' We'd go down the lane to sledge, even in the dark, the white of the snow making it seem like day time. Sometimes I would trudge back frozen stiff with wet feet at ten o'clock to find the fire falling into the grate and everyone going to bed. They'd call, 'No more coal on the fire tonight!'

The first sledge I had was around 1941 or 1942, I walked up to Birchencliffe and Arthur gave me his. It had thick runners on it and a big cut-off of metal at the front. It was heavy, uncomfortable and I was scared of going on it! Another time, I made a sledge out of steel rebar that I took from the cooling towers that were being built. I had to heat the rods in the fire to soften them so I could bend them and put holes through them with a poker.

Sometimes my mam would send me to the bakehouse. I liked going there for bread for breakfast – two or three teacakes. To get there, I'd go up Thistle Street then left up Leeds Road, past Blamires Mill (no lights on, but machines making a clatter), then across the road past the little sweet shop (with no sweets in it). Turning right through a passage, the bakehouse was on the right, and what a lovely place it was, with the smell of freshly baked bread, the brightness of white-washed walls, and a continuous sound like crickets. The baker would say 'just a minute', and would pull out the big oven bottom, take off all the bread, and replace it with the tins of risen dough. He would open the fire doors, stoke the fire, swill his hands, and put hot tea cakes in the bag. 'Six pence, please,' he'd say. I would go back out into the cold thinking it would be nice to be a baker.

I remember cold, frosty nights with just the room fire to heat the whole house. During the winter, when

Illustration 26: The view from Kilner Bank towards Thistle Street

Illustration 27: Kilner Bank

we had some coal, I used to bank the fire up before we went to bed, and wet it down on top with paper when it was all cinders and red hot. I'd press it down. Then when we got up in the morning, it was still lit. We just had to throw some coal on. My mother always used to say 'two bits, only two bits of coal.' That was rationed as well. When we went to bed, coats, clothes and anything else was piled on top for warmth. We'd put the light out first, then pull the blinds up to be able to see in the dark room, especially on a moonlit night. Then I'd be woken with the sound of the air raid warning siren – an intermittent howl, as opposed to the all-clear tone, which was a straight pitch. I remember Mam shouted 'Get dressed and down to the big shelter.' I got dressed, then asked 'Where's dad?' He shouted back, 'I'm not coming,' so I said I wasn't going then, and started taking off my clothes. My mam said 'You're coming,' but I said 'If dad's not going, I'm not going.' I got back into bed and listened for the German bombers – twenty or thirty minutes they would fly over, making for Liverpool or Manchester to hit the canals and shipping.

I laid there by myself (normally we were two or three to a bed), trying to think, was that a Dornier or a Junkers, and then the ack-ack guns would open up. Then, I got my clothes and shoes on and ran out into the street to watch the search lights and gun flashes off Lindley Moor. An air raid warden shouted at me to get down to the shelter but I didn't care. The bombers had already gone over, and I wanted to see the action, hoping for a plane to be hit. Afterwards, the all-clear siren sounded – a long wail, and then there was silence. But if you listened, you could still hear the guns going off towards the east coast.

It wasn't just the enemy who interrupted our sleep. I had to try and sleep with the clatter of mill looms and machinery coming from the mill sheds just 12 feet away across our back yard. Then there were the steam engines doing the shunting in the yards at Hillhouse just five minutes away, and along with that, the call of the shunters and, on foggy nights, the sound of the shunter's horn as the engine driver could not see the shunter's lantern; one blast for stop, two blasts for go-ahead, three blasts for reverse – and then, the sound of maybe three trucks hitting the buffers. Sometimes this would go on all night long. On a morning, the inside of the windows would be iced up – you couldn't see through the window for ice.

I remember a frosty clear night a week before Christmas of 1942 or thereabouts. Mam said I could only go carol-singing in the week directly before, as if I went too early, householders would just tell me to come back nearer Christmas. Sometimes we could not wait, and would go three weeks early to be met with this response. On this cold, clear night, Ken Stringer and I decided to go round the Birkby area. We always gave value – sometimes two or three or even all the verses. Big houses never gave more than a penny, whereas retired people gave two or threepence. Some would come to the door and say 'sing another' before any money was to be had.

There was a hoar frost on the roads and causeways that night. We'd done three or four streets and I may have had about one shilling and twopence. Ropey had ten pence (I had a better voice). As often as not, people would not answer the door. We knew it must be getting late as we hadn't set off until after eight. We decided to do one more street – we needed three bob to split it, one and sixpence each, and go home rich. We got halfway up the next street and the sirens went. We had seen the bomber's moon, so we were not surprised, and we decided to do just one more house each before the enemy aircraft came. We agreed on ten minutes, as we could hear the ack-ack guns open up to the east, and people were dashing out to shelters, and the air raid wardens were shouting for people to get off the street. We were well up Halifax Road, and it was a fifteen-minute run home, when we heard the German bombers and saw the search lights from the Lindley Moor area, like bright pencils of light in the sky. Then the heavy anti-aircraft guns opened up and we thought they were bombs – we'd heard the guns before, but never that close up. Me and Ropey went belly-splash on the causeway, which was the correct thing to do in a bombing (so as to avoid flying shrapnel) but after about two minutes we realised it was the big guns. When they stopped, other guns further away started firing, and up we got and ran home like hell – where I got a telling-off for being out in an air raid. Ropey got a telling-off from his mam too (he did not have a dad).

Dark winter nights were best for doing mischief as you could not be seen. Our gang – Acky, me, Fisher, Ropey, Brod and Pete – would go to the bottom of Gaswork Street on cold nights and stand with our backsides up against the big steel doors. Behind the doors were the town rubbish fires and it was the warmest place to be – even warmer than at home as coal was always short and it was cheaper to go to bed at nine-thirty rather than put another piece of coal on the fire.

Because coal was in short supply, I used to have to queue for coke at the gasworks. I'd get a load in a bag and put it on my lorry cart and drag it back to Thistle Street. And then my dad would make me go back – and there was always a long queue – and get coke for other people. Now and then I got tuppence for dragging coke for people on the lorry cart. I made that cart myself, and was lucky to get hold of four pram wheels for it. The cart bust eventually – a wheel came off, and I said to one of the other lads, 'come with us and help', and I put some string round the little axle and we walked right on to the gas works holding the corner up, and then all the way back with the coke loaded on, still holding the corner of the cart up with the string. The lorry cart got left after that. You'd no chance of getting any more wheels anywhere.

As mam was always sick, I had to go and stay with Grandma Evans or Grandma Roebuck. I did not mind, except I missed all my friends and I did not like the schools at either Elland or Longwood and could not wait to get out of them. I did have cousins at Elland, and there was a boy my age who lived at no.1 High Street at Longwood – he was John Haigh, and his father played an instrument in Golcar brass band – but they were not allowed to run free so it was no fun. If I was at Longwood, I would help myGranddad in the allotment, feeding the hens and digging for victory, or my Granddad and I would walk on Longwood Edge and collect horse muck for the garden. It was good when my uncle Harold came home on leave – he took me to the service men's club in town where there was pop to drink and snooker to play, or we'd go to the Dusty Miller where I had to sit outside. Before Harold went into the army, and our family used to gather in Longwood on Sundays, his mates and my dad would ride his motorbike up and down the steep stony lane to High Street, and up to Longwood Edge. Relatives used to come over from Stocksbridge too. Once my Grandma took me to see Harold at a house and he was with a woman I think was his wife. I remember one table, two chairs, a side-board, a rug. I never saw her again.

At Elland, I was with Grandma Evans, who still spoke with her heavy Scouse accent. Aunty Marie lived (or ruled) next door with all her kids. She spoke like Grandma did, and looking back, my sister Audrey was a chip off Aunty Marie. We would go to the town hall pictures or to the Rex cinema. I liked going to the Bazaar in Elland, with its bright lights and all kinds of stuff, including wind-up toys.

Illustration 28: The Bazaar in Elland

At home during the summer holidays, we would go up to Greenhead park. Two or three of us would take a bottle of water or Spanish juice, a sandwich in a bag, a home-made fishing net tied to a cane, and a jam jar with a string handle for collecting tiddlers and frog spawn from the fish pond. There were always shows, talent contests, and the paddling pool. As we had no towels, we would run round to get dry. We always got wet-through clothes, and splashed the girls who would run off screaming while we caused mayhem.

Also on summer days, we could take a trolley bus ride. The bus ran from Bradley to Marsden. We'd get on at the top of Thistle Street for threepence and get to Marsden where we'd walk about a mile to Blake Lea and swim in the deepest pools or build a dam. Or, we would get off the bus at Slaithwaite and walk up the canal bank to where the water was clean and we could dive off the lock gates. Some older lads went up to Sparth reservoir to swim, but us younger lads knew it was very cold. I did swim there years later, when I was married, and I did get cramp!

The main worry on these trips was getting money for the bus fares. The reward for taking people's empty bottles back was to keep the money and even though this was only pennies, it was a welcome way of earning something. Guinness bottles were the best - three pennies back! Digging them up off the tip was like digging up gold.

Later, I had my morning paper round, but because of that I was always a bit late to school, and I was always last to have breakfast – sometimes the jam was done, and the milk too, so I was left with tea, and bread and butter with a sprinkling of sugar. Despite being last in and first out at school, I always did well in English lessons – reading and writing – but really I finished up a dunce, and could not wait to leave school and start earning money.

I had always wanted to be a paper boy, but my dad had said I would have to be ten and have a push bike. When I was nearing ten, he did bring home a bike. It was a bone shaker, but it had solid tyres, sit-up-and-beg handlebars and one handbrake to the front wheel. The light bracket on it was great – a big brass headlight run off carbide and water. The whole thing was a museum piece but to me it was great. It had a 26 inch frame so to start with, I used it like a scooter and then I took it down the lane, put it against the big fence and climbed on. Pushing off with one hand got me rolling, but my feet did not touch the pedals. To stop, I applied the brake and laid the bike down. In this way, with plenty of cuts and bruises, I learned to ride a two-wheeler.

My dad did me proud then and got me a Claud Buttler with curved forks and drop handlebars. It was in need of an overhaul and a lick of paint, so I painted the frame and put in some new ball bearings and new brake blocks. Then up I went to Dransfields paper shop, looking for a job. They paid the best, but they had no vacancies. He put my name down, and I went on to the shop at the end of St Andrews Road where they gave me a start – 90 to 100 papers an evening for four shillings. I had to collect the money on Fridays, and if it was any short, it came out of my money. On my third or fourth week I was ninepence short so I went home with three and threepence. My dad was furious. He swore about my employer and went to knock his block off. I had never heard my dad swear – swearing was not allowed in our house. He came back with my ninepence and said I wasn't to go back. Later I got a job at Dransfields and stayed with them until I left school.

I was out of bed by 6.30, had a drink of water, then got my bike from the back yard and went through the top passage into Thistle Street. I rode up Leeds Road, past Beaumont Street and Fitzwilliam Street and the paper shop was on the right after the Fitzwilliam pub and the barbers shop. On dark mornings, the shop door was always open, but you had to pull back the heavy black-out curtain to get in. It smelled of new paper and newsprint. Cigarette smoke filled the small shop. A tubby, balding man sat behind the counter, cigarette in mouth, folding and numbering papers and stuffing them in my sack. He only smoked Capstan full strength, always available for him even when in short supply for everyone else – when it came to cigarettes, different rules applied to different customers; a workman would come in and ask for a named paper and five woodbines and, if he was liked and regular, a hand went under the counter and the paper packet of five was given for sixpence. If another customer was in, the boss would say 'Pashas only'. They smelled like camel shit, but were better than nothing.

My bag held about thirty papers to be delivered to houses on Northgate, Southgate, South Parade, Venn Street, Percival Street, Primitive Street, Friendly and Trades Club, then back down Northumberland Street as fast as my bike would go and back to the shop where my next bag was waiting – fifty or sixty more this time. I'd go up Fitzwilliam Street to what used to be a part of Rippon Brothers Rolls Royce workshops, converted into a soldiers' canteen. The cooks were all WAAFs. I had to get up there before the soldiers came in for their breakfast. I would spread out my papers on a table near the door and the men had to queue to buy them. Some would give me a penny a week to save them a Daily Mirror or more – there was Express, Chronicle, Yorkshire Post, Sketch, Mail, Graphic. It was always warm in the canteen and sometimes one WAAF who was my favourite (and looked like Betty Grable) would sneak me some porridge. They were not supposed to feed civilians on pain of being put on charge, so this was really nice, and in my old age I've often thought of her. I also got friends with a Cockney soldier. I would save him a Mirror and he brought me razor blades for my dad as these were not available at all – my dad would have to strop his old ones on his trouser belt. Any unsold papers, I took back to the shop, and my money had to be right, then it was home to a quick slice of bread and on to school.

My evening paper round started up Fitzwilliam Street, then Northgate, Beaumont Street, Leeds Road, on to the Town ground, Town Avenue estate, St Andrews Road, with the last paper being in my own Thistle Street. I could then put the bike away in the back yard and go out with the lads, or if it was wet, we'd use the big air raid shelter as our gang hut. On fine summer nights, we went on the river bank or the canal bank. When the barges came up, if I could, I would lead the horse, sometimes as far as Turnbridge or down to the ICI playing fields. We also went shooting canal rats with catapults or slug guns. I had a

Illustration 29: The Rippon Brothers garage

Illustration 30: Inside the Rippon Brothers garage

Webley but lead slugs were hard to get so it was mostly a catapult or sling shot. On wet nights we might go to the Picture House – that we knew as the 'ranch house' because they showed cowboy films. First house was six till eight, second was eight till ten. If we had stayed till ten, we made a dash for the door to avoid the stand for the King – the national anthem was played in all the picture houses. And if we had no money for the pictures, me and Ropey would climb through the Majestic toilet window and sneak onto the front row as it was always empty.

When it comes to holidays, my first memory is a trip to Liverpool to see all my dad's relatives. I try to think of faces and names, but I cannot remember them. The Mersey Tunnel, my dad told me, had just been built and was a great feat of engineering and expensive to drive through – two shillings and sixpence, or half a crown to get to New Brighton where there were buckets and spades and windmills and flags. My mam told me later that I got lost and was found two streets from where we were staying, sitting on a door step playing my mouth organ.

I remember also a trip to Blackpool with my Uncle Harold, having donkey rides, digging in the sand and eating candyfloss. Then there was the trip to Bridlington which took in the Flying Standard Nine. I must have been about 12 or so. It was after VE day and we loaded all the camping tackle, luggage and a bell tent into the car and made for the east coast – a journey which, in those days, was a long job.

The Easter fair in the 1940s caused great excitement. All the kids came to see it arrive. It was erected on the old Monday market square next to

Beaumont Street School. There were wagons and caravans filled with equipment for the rides and sideshows, and the big traction engine for the power plant. The Whip was the sensation; the cheapest ride, Noah's Ark. There were rifle stalls where you could shoot at Hitler and Mussolini, the coconut shy, the penny roll-down and the slots. There was the bearded woman, the peep shows, the flea circus, fortune tellers, wrestling booths, the fun house, the ghost train and the moon rocket. There were toffee apples and brandy snaps, whips and tops for the girls, and marbles for the boys. 1/- (a shilling) did not go far, I can tell you, and it was mostly lost in pennies, trying to gain more. The fair usually arrived on the Friday before Easter Monday, and it stayed till Wednesday. By the Friday, it was all gone, sometimes taking with it the older working lads, drawn by the tough travellers and the idea of going from place to place (including the seaside) and meeting all the girls who used to flock to the fairgrounds. If they ever came back, it was with tattoos on their arms and tall tales to tell about their travels. The big fairground rides at that time were mainly owned by a family called Lee – the name was painted on most of the rides and shows.

I remember we heard on the 5th November – just before victory in Europe – that they'd got some fireworks at Lepton. Everybody was chasing about for money and I managed to get two bob. I went up there and I got 24 Little Demons for my two bob – a penny apiece, they were. The other day, I was looking at a firework, a rocket one, and it was £30! Those Little Demons were bangers – very loud. Thunder Flashes were another sort, and they were the fireworks they used for training troops, because they sounded like an explosion, like a gun going off.

I wonder if any of my school friends remember one big event that sticks in my memory... The whole of Beaumont Street was on edge for about three days. It was all John Littlewood's fault. He had been bragging about our cock of the school, Harold Horsham, to some St Pat's kids, saying 'our lad can wallop your cock' (meaning the hardest and toughest lad in the school). The St Pat's kid was called Fred Bates, and all our lads knew about him. He was a boxer who in later years, we heard, was taken by promoters to Manchester to prize fight, when five pounds for staying three rounds was big money.

So the whole school was agog about this upcoming clash, even down to bets being laid – twopence being the most. Even though Horsham was top scrapper, he was not a bully and did not throw his weight about. In fact, he was an athlete – a great swimmer, and top runner who could walk on his hands. He was not the tallest, but had broad shoulders, and was fearless when told he was to fight Fred Bates. He said 'He doesn't scare me.' The fight was to take place in the corner of the school yard at Beaumont Street, thirty minutes after school time to give time for the teachers to go home. On the night of the fight, runners were out as we did not know which way they would come from Turnbridge. My lot, about ten of us, went Northgate and we saw them coming – Bates at the front of ten or twenty lads. We all dashed back and by this time the school yard was full, with Horsham stood in the middle. We shouted 'They're coming,' and there was uproar. Harold took off his jacket, rolled up his sleeves and spat on his hands. Bates pushed his way through and the crowd closed round, leaving me stood at the back. The lads were shouting 'Belt him, Harold!' and the lasses were screaming, but I couldn't see a thing. I had to fight my way through, just in time to see Harold hit Fred on the nose. There was blood all over, but Fred clouted Harold on the side of his head and he went down. He got up throwing punches, but was knocked down again and then it was chaos. Somebody hit me on the head so I kicked him on the shins and then everyone was fighting in a lump. I ran – I knew as I was one of the smallest lads in school I would have taken a licking that night. And anyway, I was late for my paper-round...

On being 14 years of age, I left school. I still had my evening paper round but I started work in the stores at Hebble Garage on Bradford Road, owned by Charles Wilkinson. There was no vacancy as yet in the garage itself, so my job was handing out tools, oil, grease, parts, booking in and out, sweeping the floor, making the tea, fetching fish and chips, and every menial job to be done. The garage canteen was no bigger than the average garden shed – maybe ten foot by six, brick-built with a table down the middle. The mechanics would all be sat down waiting for me to bring the fish and chips, orders having been placed in the morning. They would all have washed their hands in paraffin, so you can guess what the pots were like to clean – not to mention the taste of the bread!

My first weeks' wage was 19 shillings and sixpence. I would walk to my work and home in my overalls even when they were filthy and greasy – this let everyone know I was a working man. I was to get my second pair after my first wage. With one shilling and sixpence spend, and sixpence off my paper round, I felt like a millionaire. I also had the promise of a new suit, since my first long trousers were my dad's altered ones.

When I was fifteen, we had the big snows of 1947. There was one fire in the house and one cold tap – all hot water had to be boiled in kettles and pans, and the fire was only small because coal was in short supply. The outside toilet was across the yard. It was white-washed, and always kept clean and on freezing days, candles were placed by the side of the flushbox – when they were available. If it was frozen, the ice was broken and a bucket of hot water brought from the house to pour in. Newspaper was cut into squares and hung on a nail. You had to be desperate on a freezing night to go and sit on the throne – and even then it was a quick in and out.

When I was 16, I started with a rugby league team, but I didn't start playing until I was 17. My mate used to prop for me; I was the hooker. Then later I played scrum half. It was the Brackenhall team – there were new council houses there, where they'd got rid of the old terrace houses. One time, we were playing against Underbank, at Holmfirth. About five of the team went on the bus and we all had our boots wrapped round our necks, jersey and shorts stuffed in our pockets. An old boy who saw us asked, 'who are you laiking?' We told him and he warned us, if there's any fellas on the side who've got sticks, they'll trip you up while you're running down the touchline! Underbank were the top of the league, but we beat them. We scored two tries and they had a couple of goal kicks. There were no changing rooms, just a tin bath to wash in, but I had my first cup of coffee there. It wasn't coffee as you'd know it, though. It was coffee in a bottle, and they made it using acorns and all sorts. But it was a hot drink, it kept you warm.

One time, when I went playing rugby at Leeds Road, my mother said, make sure you come back here for your tea, I've got something special for you. Normally I'd get all my gear, go straight up town afterwards and go into the Square's toilets, because for 2p you could have a wash and brush up and go straight to the pictures – and you could get the papers that were coming out with all the results for racing and football and rugby in them. But this time, I went home and it was worth it. There was an egg – one egg – fried with some bread, and I relished it. I never got an egg! That was a big treat. I was 17, a working man, and a single egg was a treat.

Nowadays, when I wake up – and I am always awake early – I cannot lie in bed. If I lay back and listen, the silence is deafening and I think to myself, no one works any more; and I think about being woken up in Thistle Street – the clatter of rail engines on the main line, the clatter of looms directly behind the house, the roar of tipper wagons dropping coal at the boiler house, workers' clogs and boots on the street and the sound of hammers on steel at Moorhouse Boilers. And now, no sound. Not even a train across the valley.

Illustration 31: The playground of my youth

Illustration 32: Birchencliffe, the place of my earliest memories; a view from the junction of Cliffe Hill and Halifax Road